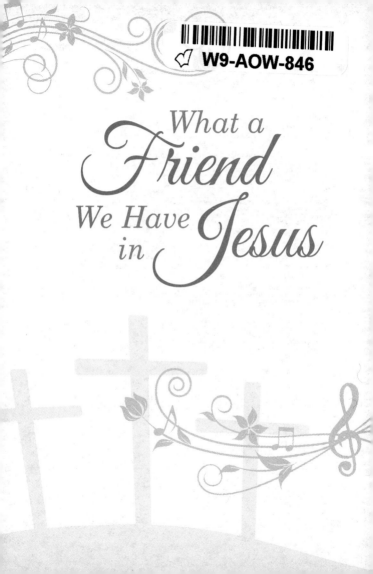

What a
Friend
We Have
in *Jesus*

© 2014 by Barbour Publishing, Inc.

Written and compiled by Emily Biggers.

Print ISBN 978-1-62416-693-8

eBook Editions:
Adobe Digital Edition (.epub) 978-1-62836-359-3
Kindle and MobiPocket Edition (.prc) 978-1-62836-360-9

Published by Barbour Publishing, Inc., P.O. Box 719, Uhrichsville, Ohio 44683, www.barbourbooks.com

Our mission is to publish and distribute inspirational products offering exceptional value and biblical encouragement to the masses.

 Member of the
Evangelical Christian
Publishers Association

Printed in the United States of America.

What a Friend We Have in Jesus

Inspiration from the Beloved Hymn

BARBOUR
PUBLISHING

Contents

What a Friend We Have in Jesus

What a friend we have in Jesus,
all our sins and griefs to bear!
What a privilege to carry
everything to God in prayer!
O what peace we often forfeit,
O what needless pain we bear,
all because we do not carry
everything to God in prayer.

Have we trials and temptations?
Is there trouble anywhere?
We should never be discouraged;
take it to the Lord in prayer.
Can we find a friend so faithful
who will all our sorrows share?
Jesus knows our every weakness;
take it to the Lord in prayer.

Are we weak and heavy laden,
cumbered with a load of care?
Precious Savior, still our refuge,
take it to the Lord in prayer.
Do your friends despise, forsake you?
Take it to the Lord in prayer!
In His arms He'll take and shield you;
you will find a solace there.

Blessed Savior, Thou hast promised
Thou wilt all our burdens bear
may we ever, Lord, be bringing
all to Thee in earnest prayer.
Soon in glory bright unclouded
there will be no need for prayer
rapture, praise and endless worship
will be our sweet portion there.

Lyrics by Joseph M. Scriven, 1855

What a Friend!

"Greater love has no one than this:
to lay down one's life for one's friends."
JOHN 15:13 NIV

When Jesus died on the cross, He died once
and for all. He willingly laid down His life for
mankind. Certainly other men have died in
order to save the life of another. Soldiers in
battle, firefighters and other first responders
to tragedies. But Christ chose His death. He
died to fulfill the requirement of the sacrifice
of a lamb. His blood was graciously shed to
atone for our sins. He left the glory of heaven
in order to come to earth and experience life as
a man. Fully God and yet fully man, He went
to the cross and offered up His perfect life so
that sinners might have abundant and eternal
life. He did not die for the righteous but for the
unrighteous. His death and resurrection is the
bridge for us to commune with our holy God.

And so, in the midst of great joy and on
your darkest day, remember that you have
a friend in Jesus. He is the best friend you
could ever ask for, faithful and loving to the end.
He bore every sin you have ever and will ever
commit when He hung on that old rugged cross.
And He did not stay in the tomb. Jesus is alive!
He sits at the right hand of the Father and
He lives in your heart. He wants to bear
your sorrows for you. Call upon the name
of Jesus. He is a friend like no other.

*No longer do I call you servants, for the servant
does not know what his master is doing; but I
have called you friends, for all that I have heard
from my Father I have made known to you.*

JOHN 15:15 ESV

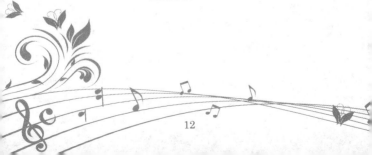

*"Behold, I stand at the door and knock; if anyone
hears My voice and opens the door, I will come in
to him and will dine with him, and he with Me."*

REVELATION 3:20 NASB

*When Jesus saw their faith, he said,
"Friend, your sins are forgiven."*

LUKE 5:20 NIV

No one else holds or has held the place in
the heart of the world which Jesus holds.
Other gods have been as devoutly worshipped;
no other man has been so devoutly loved.

JOHN KNOX

A friend is a person with whom I may be
sincere. Before him I may think aloud.

RALPH WALDO EMERSON

There is a brotherhood within the body of
believers, and the Lord Jesus Christ is the
common denominator. Friendship and
fellowship are the legal tender among believers.

J. VERNON MCGEE

Hold a true friend with both your hands.

NIGERIAN PROVERB

See what great love the Father has lavished on us, that we should be called children of God!

1 JOHN 3:1 NIV

Jesus told him, "I am the way, the truth, and the life. No one can come to the Father except through me."

JOHN 14:6 NLT

For you have not received a spirit of slavery leading to fear again, but you have received a spirit of adoption as sons by which we cry out, "Abba! Father!"

ROMANS 8:15 NASB

"And surely I am with you always, to the very end of the age."

MATTHEW 28:20 NIV

Savior and Friend

On my best days as well as my worst days,
I look around for a friend. I want someone
with whom I can share the good news and the
bad. I need someone who understands me,
who sympathizes with me, who cares.
That friend is You, Jesus. I know that no
one else can fill the spot in my heart that is
designed for You. I am so thankful to have
You as my Savior and friend. Amen.

*For we do not have a high priest who is
unable to sympathize with our weaknesses,
but one who in every respect has been
tempted as we are, yet without sin.*

HEBREWS 4:15 ESV

*And so it happened just as the Scriptures say:
"Abraham believed God, and God counted
him as righteous because of his faith."
He was even called the friend of God.*

JAMES 2:23 NLT

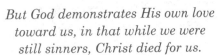

*But God demonstrates His own love
toward us, in that while we were
still sinners, Christ died for us.*

ROMANS 5:8 NKJV

I have read in Plato and Cicero sayings
that are very wise and very beautiful; but I
never read in either of them: "Come unto me
all ye that labour and are heavy laden."

AUGUSTINE

Walking with a friend in the dark is
better than walking alone in the light.

HELEN KELLER

There is only one secure foundation:
a genuine, deep relationship with Jesus Christ,
which will carry you through any and all
turmoil. No matter what storms are
raging all around, you'll stand firm if
you stand on His love.

CHARLES STANLEY

*"You are my friends if you do
what I command you."*

JOHN 15:14 ESV

*For I am convinced that neither death
nor life, neither angels nor demons, neither
the present nor the future, nor any powers,
neither height nor depth, nor anything else in
all creation, will be able to separate us from the
love of God that is in Christ Jesus our Lord.*

ROMANS 8:38–39 NIV

*For there is one God and one mediator between
God and mankind, the man Christ Jesus,
who gave himself as a ransom for all people.*

1 TIMOTHY 2:5–6 NIV

Sweet Fellowship

Lord Jesus, thank You for being my
very best friend. It amazes me that in all
Your glory and righteousness, You chose
to die on a cross for my sins to set me free.
You have given me abundant life on this earth
and the promise of eternal life with You in
heaven. Help me to walk and talk with You in
sweet fellowship and friendship every day.
I love You, Lord. Amen.

There is a God-shaped vacuum in the heart
of every man which cannot be filled by any
created thing, but only by God, the Creator,
made known through Jesus.

BLAISE PASCAL

A rule I have had for years is: to treat
the Lord Jesus Christ as a personal friend.
His is not a creed, a mere doctrine,
but it is He Himself we have.

D. L. MOODY

Love is the only force capable of
transforming an enemy into friend.

MARTIN LUTHER KING JR.

A friend is one who knows you
and loves you just the same.

ELBERT HUBBARD

The Privilege of Prayer

*Rejoice always, pray continually,
give thanks in all circumstances; for this is
God's will for you in Christ Jesus.*

1 Thessalonians 5:16–18 niv

Prayer is not optional. God calls His children to pray constantly, in all circumstances—good and bad alike. The believer would be foolish not to accept the gift and exercise the great privilege of prayer. Through Jesus, Christians are able to commune with the God of the universe. Prayer is the avenue through which we praise the Lord, thank Him, ask Him for specific needs to be met, and lift others up to Him. The Bible tells us to cast our cares on the Lord because He cares for us. How comforting to know that we have a place to turn and someone who is always there, ready to listen and guide.

If you have not been taking advantage of the privilege of prayer, begin today. It is never too late to begin talking with your Father. Start by expressing to God how much you love Him. Thank Him for all that He has done and all that He is going to do. Go before Him boldly, remembering that your words are not bouncing off the ceiling but being heard by your loving heavenly Father. Prayer is a privilege that is granted to every single believer in Jesus Christ. Pray in the powerful name of Jesus, and watch as your prayers are answered.

This is the confidence we have in approaching God: that if we ask anything according to his will, he hears us. And if we know that he hears us—whatever we ask—we know that we have what we asked of him.

1 JOHN 5:14–15 NIV

Do not be anxious about anything, but in every situation, by prayer and petition, with thanksgiving, present your requests to God. And the peace of God, which transcends all understanding, will guard your hearts and your minds in Christ Jesus.

PHILIPPIANS 4:6–7 NIV

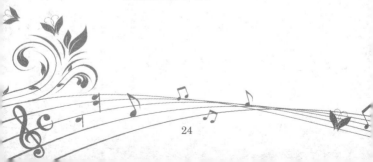

Prayer is as natural an expression
of faith as breathing is of life.

JONATHAN EDWARDS

I have so much to do that I shall
spend the first three hours in prayer.

MARTIN LUTHER

We have to pray with our eyes on God,
not on the difficulties.

OSWALD CHAMBERS

He who knows how to overcome with God in
prayer has heaven and earth at his disposal.

CHARLES SPURGEON

*One of those days Jesus went out to a
mountainside to pray, and spent
the night praying to God.*

LUKE 6:12 NIV

*"But you, when you pray, go into your room,
and when you have shut your door, pray to your
Father who is in the secret place; and your Father
who sees in secret will reward you openly."*

MATTHEW 6:6 NKJV

*Is anyone among you in trouble? Let them pray.
Is anyone happy? Let them sing songs of praise.*

JAMES 5:13 NIV

A Desire to Pray

Why is it so hard for me to pray, Lord?
My mind wanders, and sometimes I wonder
if You even hear my words. Father, I want
to be faithful in prayer. I know that intimate
fellowship only comes as a result of time spent
together. Create in me a desire to pray, and
remind me of the wonderful privilege I have
been given that I might converse with the
God of the universe! Amen.

*The L*ORD *is near to all who call upon Him,*
To all who call upon Him in truth.

PSALM 145:18 NKJV

If you need wisdom, ask our generous God, and
he will give it to you. He will not rebuke you for
asking. But when you ask him, be sure that your
faith is in God alone. Do not waver, for a person
with divided loyalty is as unsettled as a wave of
the sea that is blown and tossed by the wind.

JAMES 1:5–6 NLT

Prayer means that I come in contact with
an almighty Christ, and almighty results
happen along the lines He laid down.

OSWALD CHAMBERS

Faith sees the invisible, believes the
unbelievable, and receives the impossible.

CORRIE TEN BOOM

Avail yourself of the greatest privilege
this side of heaven. Jesus Christ died to
make this communion and communication
with the Father possible.

BILLY GRAHAM

Wise is he in the day of trouble who knows his
true source of strength and who fails not to pray.

E. M. BOUNDS

The earnest prayer of a righteous person has
great power and produces wonderful results.
JAMES 5:16 NLT

"Call upon Me in the day of trouble;
I will deliver you, and you shall glorify Me."
PSALM 50:15 NKJV

Create in me a pure heart, O God,
and renew a steadfast spirit within me.
PSALM 51:10 NIV

Cast all your anxiety on him
because he cares for you.
1 PETER 5:7 NIV

Give It to God

Father, I give You my burdens. I cast them down
before You because You have told me that it is
all right to do so. I come before You heavy laden,
but I rise to face the day unencumbered. I refuse
to gather up the worries that I have trusted You
with and cling to them any longer. You are big
enough to handle anything that comes my way.
Guide me and take care of me, I pray.

True prayer is measured by weight, not by length. A single groan before God may have more fullness of prayer in it than a fine oration.

CHARLES SPURGEON

Just as the business of the tailor is to make clothes, and that of the shoemaker to mend shoes, so the business of the Christian is to pray.

MARTIN LUTHER

Prayer is asking for rain.
Faith is carrying the umbrella.

ROBERT C. SAVAGE

What wings are to a bird, and sails to a ship, prayer is to the soul.

CORRIE TEN BOOM

Forfeited Peace

For to set the mind on the flesh is death,
but to set the mind on the Spirit is life and peace.

ROMANS 8:6 ESV

Every elementary school student learns about opposites. Hot and cold. Up and down. Light versus dark. But have you considered the opposite of peace? Who wants to live a life filled with turmoil and anxiety? Imagine the ocean in all her might crashing in upon the shore again and again as a wild tropical storm devours a row of pristine beach houses. The wind howls all around you. You try to run but it knocks you to your knees. The pelting rain blinds you. Your heart pounds within your chest as you cling to life, hoping only to survive. *Turmoil.* Now force your mind to dwell on the opposite. Gentle waves lap at the shore. A gulf breeze blows. You walk in silence along the coastline, dipping your toes in the cool water, turning your face to the warmth of the sun. *Peace.*

Each day you make a choice between the calm and the storm, between—as scripture declares—life and death. Do you set your mind on the things of this world? Are you so caught up in work or relationships that you have squeezed God out of your heart? So many Christians forfeit the peace God intends for them to possess. Focus on the Holy Spirit. He is your comforter and counselor. Jesus asked the Father to send Him to you that you might live a life of peace, not distress. Make a conscious choice today to set your mind on the Spirit. Peace is just a prayer away.

I have set the LORD continually before me;
because He is at my right hand,
I will not be shaken.

PSALM 16:8 NASB

And the peace of God, which transcends
all understanding, will guard your hearts
and your minds in Christ Jesus.

PHILIPPIANS 4:7 NIV

"Peace I leave with you; my peace I give you.
I do not give to you as the world gives. Do not
let your hearts be troubled and do not be afraid."

JOHN 14:27 NIV

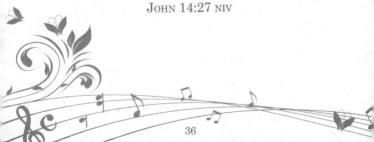

Don't pray when you feel like it.
Have an appointment with the Lord and
keep it. A man is powerful on his knees.

CORRIE TEN BOOM

Those persons who know the deep peace
of God, the unfathomable peace that
passeth all understanding, are always
men and women of much prayer.

R. A. TORREY

A great many people are trying to make
peace, but that has already been done.
God has not left it for us to do; all we
have to do is to enter into it.

D. L. MOODY

You will make known to me the path of life;
in Your presence is fullness of joy; in Your
right hand there are pleasures forever.

PSALM 16:11 NASB

The LORD is near to those who have a broken
heart, and saves such as have a contrite spirit.

PSALM 34:18 NKJV

You will keep in perfect peace those whose
minds are steadfast, because they trust in you.

ISAIAH 26:3 NIV

Surrender

Lord, I toss and turn in my bed. I can't seem
to turn my mind off and rest. You are there,
aren't You, Father? You watch me wrestling
with the cares of this world and You long for
me to turn to You. You wait for me to surrender.
I am the stubborn one who tries to figure it
all out on my own. I need the peace that floods
over me when I pray. Teach me to pray.

"I have told you these things, so that
in me you may have peace. In this world
you will have trouble. But take heart!
I have overcome the world."

JOHN 16:33 NIV

"Surely God is my salvation; I will trust
and not be afraid. The LORD, the LORD
himself, is my strength and my defense;
he has become my salvation."

ISAIAH 12:2 NIV

"For God so loved the world that he gave his
one and only Son, that whoever believes in
him shall not perish but have eternal life."

JOHN 3:16 NIV

Let not your peace rest in the utterances
of men, for whether they put a good or bad
construction on your conduct does not
make you other than you are.

THOMAS À KEMPIS

If we have not quiet in our minds,
outward comfort will do no more for
us than a golden slipper on a gouty foot.

JOHN BUNYAN

Man is not at peace with his fellow man
because he is not at peace with himself;
he is not at peace with himself, because
he is not at peace with God.

THOMAS MERTON

Therefore, since we have been justified through
faith, we have peace with God through our Lord
Jesus Christ, through whom we have gained access
by faith into this grace in which we now stand.
And we boast in the hope of the glory of God.

ROMANS 5:1–2 NIV

For to us a child is born, to us a son is given,
and the government will be on his shoulders.
And he will be called Wonderful Counselor,
Mighty God, Everlasting Father, Prince of Peace.

ISAIAH 9:6 NIV

The Heart, Not the Words

God, I feel that I should use lofty, spiritual-
sounding words when I come to You in prayer.
I hear others pray with such eloquence.
Sometimes I don't pray because I don't know
what to say or how to put it into words. But I
know that You are much more interested in my
heart than in my words. Remind me that I can
come to You with anything and everything.
I love You, Lord. Amen.

God cannot give us a happiness and peace
apart from Himself, because it is not there.
There is no such thing.

C. S. Lewis

I have to get to the point of the absolute
and unquestionable relationship that takes
everything exactly as it comes from Him.
God never guides us at some time in the future,
but always here and now. Realize that the
Lord is here now, and the freedom you
receive is immediate.

Oswald Chambers

We should have much more peace if
we would not busy ourselves with
the sayings and doings of others.

Thomas à Kempis

Trials and Temptations

No temptation has overtaken you except what is common to mankind. And God is faithful; he will not let you be tempted beyond what you can bear. But when you are tempted, he will also provide a way out so that you can endure it.

1 CORINTHIANS 10:13 NIV

Life is a maze. Trying to find your way around the corners and avoiding bumping into dead ends can be quite the challenge! Do you find yourself hitting the same wall again and again in life? Are you continuously tempted to travel in a direction that you know is not God's best? Is there a trial that weighs on you, holding you back from the freedom you once knew in Christ? God is still there. He is faithful to His children. He will never give you more than you can bear. If there is a great struggle in your life, God knows you will be able to overcome.

It will take time and constant surrender to the Lord, but you will get beyond it. If there are temptations that nip at your ankles, demanding your attention, be done with them! Give them to God. You may have to pray daily to receive the strength to resist them. Hourly even. But God stands ready to save you. He desires that none of His children should give in to the clever traps of Satan.

Life is a maze. That is certain. But God offers you a hand to hold as you navigate its twists and turns. Ask Him for help. He is waiting to see if you are willing to accept it. He knows how to get you from point A to point B. Let God show you the way out.

"Watch and pray, lest you enter into temptation. The spirit indeed is willing, but the flesh is weak."

MATTHEW 26:41 NKJV

Those who want to get rich fall into temptation and a trap and into many foolish and harmful desires that plunge people into ruin and destruction.

1 TIMOTHY 6:9 NIV

Consider it pure joy, my brothers and sisters, whenever you face trials of many kinds, because you know that the testing of your faith produces perseverance. Let perseverance finish its work so that you may be mature and complete, not lacking anything.

JAMES 1:2–4 NIV

What would you expect? Sin will not come to you, saying, "I am sin." It would do little harm if it did. Sin always seems "good, and pleasant, and desirable," at the time of commission.

JAMES CHARLES RYLE

It does not matter how small the sins are, provided their cumulative effect is to edge the man (or the woman) away from the light and out into the Nothing. Murder is no better than cards, if cards can do the trick. Indeed, the safest road to hell is the gradual one.

C. S. LEWIS

"And do not lead us into temptation, but deliver us from the evil one. For Yours is the kingdom and the power and the glory forever. Amen."

MATTHEW 6:13 NKJV

In all this you greatly rejoice, though now for a little while you may have had to suffer grief in all kinds of trials. These have come so that the proven genuineness of your faith—of greater worth than gold, which perishes even though refined by fire—may result in praise, glory and honor when Jesus Christ is revealed.

1 PETER 1:6–7 NIV

A Gentle Hand

This one particular trial almost has me beaten, God. I am just not strong enough. It is too difficult to face, too powerful to conquer, too sad to endure. But You, oh Lord, are stronger than even my greatest struggle. It is not too hard for You. You are a mighty warrior ready to go to battle for my soul. And yet, You also wipe away my tears with a gentle hand. Lord, I need You so. Amen.

*Blessed is the one who perseveres under trial
because, having stood the test, that person
will receive the crown of life that the Lord has
promised to those who love him.*

JAMES 1:12 NIV

*"As surely as I valued your life today,
so may the LORD value my life and
deliver me from all trouble."*

1 SAMUEL 26:24 NIV

*Many are the afflictions of the righteous,
but the LORD delivers him out of them all.*

PSALM 34:19 NASB

Do not suppose that abuses are eliminated
by destroying the object which is abused.
Men can go wrong with wine and women.
Shall we prohibit and abolish women? The sun,
moon, and stars have been worshipped.
Shall we pluck them out of the sky?

MARTIN LUTHER

Never deliberate what is clearly wrong,
and try to persuade yourself that it is not.

FREDERICK TEMPLE

We have no sufficient strength of our own.
All our sufficiency is of God. We should stir
up ourselves to resist temptations in a
reliance upon God's all-sufficiency and
the omnipotence of His might.

MATTHEW HENRY

Submit therefore to God. Resist the
devil and he will flee from you.

JAMES 4:7 NASB

But the fruit of the Spirit is love, joy,
peace, patience, kindness, goodness,
faithfulness, gentleness, self-control;
against such things there is no law.

GALATIANS 5:22–23 NASB

Rejoicing in hope, persevering in
tribulation, devoted to prayer. . .

ROMANS 12:12 NASB

He who overcomes, I will grant to him to sit
down with Me on My throne, as I also overcame
and sat down with My Father on His throne.

REVELATION 3:21 NASB

Power Source

Father, the same temptations come back again and again in my life. Just when I think I have them under control, they sneak up on me once more. Give me the strength to say no to things that are not Your will. I do not have the power on my own. It has to come from You. I choose to tap into Your strength through prayer. Help me to resist the temptation to sin against You. Amen.

Unwillingness to accept God's "way of
escape" from temptation frightens me—
what a rebel yet resides within.

JIM ELLIOT

Temptations and occasions put nothing into a
man, but only draw out what was in him before.

JOHN OWEN

Flee temptation and don't
leave a forwarding address.

UNKNOWN

Satan gives Adam an apple, and takes
away Paradise. Therefore in all temptations
let us consider not what he offers,
but what we shall lose.

RICHARD SIBBES

Trouble in This Life

"Behold, I am doing a new thing; now it springs forth, do you not perceive it? I will make a way in the wilderness and rivers in the desert."

ISAIAH 43:19 ESV

Solomon, one of the wisest men who ever lived, concludes in the book of Ecclesiastes that life is hard. He finds it all meaningless, in fact. Every generation will experience loss, disappointment, and trials. Ever since Adam and Eve tasted of the forbidden fruit in Eden, this world has been less than perfect. So, it's a given. We live and breathe and make our way in a fallen world every moment from birth until the last breath we take in these shells. Sounds like bad news, doesn't it? But there is always good news with Jesus!

The Bible declares that in Christ we are more than conquerors. It proclaims that in Him we can do all things. The words of the holy scriptures advise us not to worry about the troubles we will face in the future but to let each day unfold in its own time. Trust God. He is doing a new thing in your life! He is making a way through the trouble to the other side. Did He not prove that He is able when He parted the Red Sea and allowed His children to cross it? The Egyptians were caught up in the waters and drowned just as the last Israelite planted his foot on the safe shoreline. Face the inevitable troubles of this life with your sovereign God.

*But understand this, that in the last days there
will come times of difficulty. For people will be
lovers of self, lovers of money, proud, arrogant,
abusive, disobedient to their parents, ungrateful,
unholy, heartless, unappeasable, slanderous,
without self-control, brutal, not loving good,
treacherous, reckless, swollen with conceit, lovers
of pleasure rather than lovers of God, having the
appearance of godliness, but denying its power.*

2 TIMOTHY 3:1–5 ESV

*"I have said these things to you, that in
me you may have peace. In the world
you will have tribulation. But take heart;
I have overcome the world."*

JOHN 16:33 ESV

Unless we form the habit of going to the Bible in bright moments as well as in trouble, we cannot fully respond to its consolations because we lack equilibrium between light and darkness.

HELEN KELLER

Expect trouble as an inevitable part
of life and repeat to yourself, the most
comforting words of all; this, too, shall pass.

ANN LANDERS

There are always uncertainties ahead,
but there is always one certainty—
God's will is good.

VERNON PATERSON

"Let not your hearts be troubled. Believe in God; believe also in me. In my Father's house are many rooms. If it were not so, would I have told you that I go to prepare a place for you? And if I go and prepare a place for you, I will come again and will take you to myself, that where I am you may be also."

JOHN 14:1–3 ESV

For everyone who has been born of God overcomes the world. And this is the victory that has overcome the world—our faith.

1 JOHN 5:4 ESV

No More Trouble

Lord, I am looking forward to the day when there will be no more trials or struggles of any type. There will be no more tears, no more sadness, no more grief. I am thankful for the promise of eternal life in heaven where all things will be right and good. In the meantime, I know that You are with me to face the trouble of each day. Thank You, Father, for Your faithfulness. Amen.

"And which of you by worrying
can add one cubit to his stature?"
Luke 12:25 nkjv

There is a way which seems right to a man,
but its end is the way of death.
Proverbs 14:12 nasb

"So do not worry about tomorrow;
for tomorrow will care for itself.
Each day has enough trouble of its own."
Matthew 6:34 nasb

But even if you should suffer for what
is right, you are blessed. "Do not fear
their threats; do not be frightened."
1 Peter 3:14 niv

I'm taking the Lord at His word, and I'm
trusting Him to prove His Word. It's kind of like
putting all your eggs in one basket, but we've
already put our trust in Him for salvation, so
why not do it as far as our life is concerned?

ED McCULLY

God has wisely kept us in the dark concerning
future events and reserved for Himself the
knowledge of them, that He may train us
up in a dependence upon Himself and a
continued readiness for every event.

MATTHEW HENRY

When trouble comes, focus on
God's ability to care for you.

CHARLES STANLEY

Do not be conformed to this world, but be transformed by the renewal of your mind, that by testing you may discern what is the will of God, what is good and acceptable and perfect.

ROMANS 12:2 ESV

Be alert and of sober mind. Your enemy the devil prowls around like a roaring lion looking for someone to devour.

1 PETER 5:8 NIV

But you belong to God, my dear children. You have already won a victory over those people, because the Spirit who lives in you is greater than the spirit who lives in the world.

1 JOHN 4:4 NLT

Struggling with Struggles

I feel overwhelmed, God. I admit it. My troubles
do not feel momentary, and I do not feel joyful
in my trials. Honestly, I struggle to understand
why You allow them. It feels good to come before
You and share with You that this is hard and
I am weak. Promise to be with me, Father.
Walk with me. Guide me. I can only face these
troubles in the shelter of Your wings. Amen.

God is God. Because He is God, He is worthy of my trust and obedience. I will find rest nowhere but in His holy will, a will that is unspeakably beyond my largest notions of what He is up to.

ELISABETH ELLIOT

God will never, never, never let us down if we have faith and put our trust in Him. He will always look after us. So we must cleave to Jesus. Our whole life must simply be woven into Jesus.

MOTHER TERESA

Don't trust to hold God's hand;
let Him hold yours. Let Him do
the holding, and you the trusting.

HAMMER WILLIAM WEBB-PEPLOE

Be Encouraged!

> *"The LORD himself goes before you and will be with you; he will never leave you nor forsake you. Do not be afraid; do not be discouraged."*
>
> DEUTERONOMY 31:8 NIV

Do not be afraid. Do not be dismayed. Do not be discouraged. These words appear regularly in the Bible. Often they were spoken before soldiers went into battle as a reminder that God was going ahead of them and they had nothing to fear in their enemies. Every day as believers, we fight a spiritual battle against the prince of this world, Satan. These words are not suggestions. They are *commands*. And yet many Christians find themselves stuck deep down in the mire of fear and discouragement. What causes followers of Christ to lose sight of the fact that God has it all under control? Could it be that they forget to take their worries to the Lord in prayer?

Remember running to a parent or grandparent when you were a child? If you had good news to share, you wanted to get to that person as quickly as possible in order to share it. If you were hurt or sad, you could hardly wait to be wrapped up in a safe embrace. This is how it should be between you and your heavenly Father. Whatever is troubling you today, wait no longer to run to Him. Do not be discouraged! He is a great big God, and you only need to make your way into His loving arms to remember that He is the source of all joy and encouragement.

The name of the LORD is a strong tower;
the righteous run to it and are safe.

PROVERBS 18:10 NKJV

Trust in the LORD with all your heart and
do not lean on your own understanding.
In all your ways acknowledge Him,
and He will make your paths straight.

PROVERBS 3:5–6 NASB

"So do not fear, for I am with you;
do not be dismayed, for I am your God.
I will strengthen you and help you; I will
uphold you with my righteous right hand."

ISAIAH 41:10 NIV

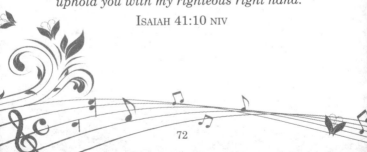

Encouragement from God

Lord, encourage my heart today as only You
can do. I need to sense that I am deeply loved.
The worries and pressures of the world could
easily discourage were it not for the intimate
fellowship I share with You. No matter what
comes my way, You will be steadfast and true.
With You on my side, nothing can overtake
me or steal my joy. Thank You, Lord,
for loving me the way that You do. Amen.

God is our refuge and strength, always ready to help in times of trouble. So we will not fear when earthquakes come and the mountains crumble into the sea. Let the oceans roar and foam. Let the mountains tremble as the waters surge!

PSALM 46:1–3 NLT

My comfort in my suffering is this:
your promise preserves my life.

PSALM 119:50 NIV

Likewise the Spirit helps us in our weakness. For we do not know what to pray for as we ought, but the Spirit himself intercedes for us with groanings too deep for words.

ROMANS 8:26 ESV

I would go to the deeps a hundred times to cheer a downcast spirit. It is good for me to have been afflicted, that I might know how to speak a word in season to one that is weary.

CHARLES SPURGEON

Discouraged not by difficulties without, or the anguish of ages within, the heart listens to a secret voice that whispers: "Be not dismayed; in the future lies the Promised Land."

HELEN KELLER

God hath made it a debt which one saint owes to another to carry their names to a throne of grace.

WILLIAM GURNALL

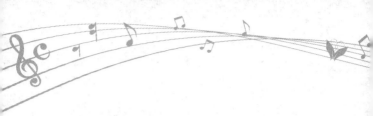

May the God of hope fill you with all joy and peace in believing, so that by the power of the Holy Spirit you may abound in hope.

ROMANS 15:13 ESV

But he said to me, "My grace is sufficient for you, for my power is made perfect in weakness." Therefore I will boast all the more gladly of my weaknesses, so that the power of Christ may rest upon me.

2 CORINTHIANS 12:9 ESV

"Have I not commanded you? Be strong and courageous. Do not be afraid; do not be discouraged, for the LORD your God will be with you wherever you go."

JOSHUA 1:9 NIV

Contentment in Christ

As a Christian, Lord, I have such an advantage.
When the world drags me down, I can slip away
and meet with my Creator. I am in this world,
but not of it. I am set apart as a beloved daughter
of the King. I do not seek encouragement from
the world because it offers me no contentment.
My worth is found in Jesus Christ alone. Lift my
spirits, Father, as I bask in Your presence.

"The thief comes only to steal and kill and
destroy. I came that they may have
life and have it abundantly."

JOHN 10:10 ESV

*For this light momentary affliction is preparing
for us an eternal weight of glory beyond all
comparison, as we look not to the things that are
seen but to the things that are unseen. For the
things that are seen are transient, but the
things that are unseen are eternal.*

2 CORINTHIANS 4:17–18 ESV

When it seems as if God is far away, remind
yourself that He is near. Nearness is not a
matter of geography. God is everywhere.
Nearness is likeness. The more we become
like the Lord, the nearer He is to us.

WARREN WIERSBE

Nothing but encouragement can come to us as we
dwell upon the faithful dealing of our heavenly
Father in centuries gone by. Faith in God has not
saved people from hardships and trials, but it has
enabled them to bear tribulations courageously
and to emerge victoriously.

LEIGH ROBERSON

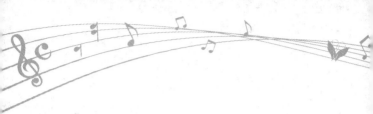

*Be strong, and let your heart take courage,
all you who wait for the Lord!*
PSALM 31:24 ESV

*Therefore encourage one another and build
up one another, just as you also are doing.*
1 THESSALONIANS 5:11 NASB

*"These things I have spoken to you, that my joy
may be in you, and that your joy may be full."*
JOHN 15:11 ESV

*But exhort one another every day, as long
as it is called "today," that none of you may
be hardened by the deceitfulness of sin.*
HEBREWS 3:13 ESV

Take It to the Lord

Father, I am so busy telling everyone else my
troubles I often forget to come to You in prayer.
You are the one who knows me and loves me
best. It's no wonder I feel discouraged. I am
seeking answers and comfort from others when
I should be at my Father's feet. Help me to
remember the peace that fills my spirit when
I spend time in prayer. I am refreshed and
renewed in Your presence, Lord. Amen.

Keep your face to the sunshine
and you cannot see a shadow.
HELEN KELLER

You are valuable because you exist.
Not because of what you do or what you
have done, but simply because you are.
MAX LUCADO

Be assured, if you walk with Him
and look to Him, and expect help
from Him, He will never fail you.
GEORGE MUELLER

The stars may fall, but God's
promises will stand and be fulfilled.
J. I. PACKER

Faithful Friend

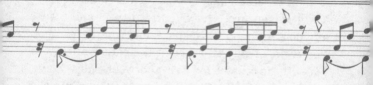

But the Lord is faithful. He will establish
you and guard you against the evil one.

2 THESSALONIANS 3:3 ESV

A faithful friend. How could I ask for more? You
are incapable of faithlessness. You are God—
all-powerful and all too aware of my sin. . .and
yet, You remain loyal to me through it all.

My life is a roller-coaster ride. In my
humanity, emotions take me up and down. It is
a wild adventure! And yet, after I twist and turn
and do a few loop the loops, I find You there.
You stand steady and true at the gate, waiting.
I get off the coaster for a rest between rides. You
take my hand. We walk for a while. You remind
me that I am Your child and You are my Father,
this life on earth is temporary, and these trials
shall pass just as the last ones did.

Alas, another ride is inevitable. You help me buckle my seat belt. And You do an amazing thing! You take the seat beside me. We ride together. I scream for joy. . .and then from sheer terror. Life is funny that way. Up and down we go, faster, faster. . .I look to You. You are not screaming or afraid. You are not thrown off balance or shaken. You know it all comes out okay in the end. I take Your hand and squeeze it hard. You don't seem to mind. Thank You, Lord, for riding with me, for holding me steady, for being faithful. Your love amazes me.

*"Know therefore that the LORD your God is
God, the faithful God who keeps covenant and
steadfast love with those who love him and keep
his commandments, to a thousand generations."*

DEUTERONOMY 7:9 ESV

*God is faithful, by whom you were called into the
fellowship of His Son, Jesus Christ our Lord.*

1 CORINTHIANS 1:9 NKJV

*For the word of the LORD is right
and true; he is faithful in all he does.*

PSALM 33:4 NIV

*If we are faithless, he remains
faithful—for he cannot deny himself.*

2 TIMOTHY 2:13 ESV

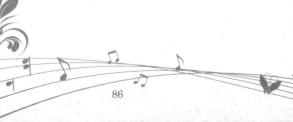

Faithful Friend

Jesus, You are so faithful to me. Even the
dearest of men and women will let me down.
They are only human. But You are loyal and
true at all times. You never change. You are
the same yesterday, today, and tomorrow.
I am thankful for a friend who will never leave
me. You willingly bear my burdens just as
You bore my sins on the cross of Calvary.
I love You, Lord. Amen.

If we confess our sins, he is faithful and just to forgive us our sins and to cleanse us from all unrighteousness.

1 John 1:9 esv

"Therefore do not be anxious, saying, 'What shall we eat?' or 'What shall we drink?' or 'What shall we wear?' For the Gentiles seek after all these things, and your heavenly Father knows that you need them all. But seek first the kingdom of God and his righteousness, and all these things will be added to you."

Matthew 6:31–33 esv

God is not a deceiver, that He should
offer to support us, and then, when we lean
upon Him, should slip away from us.

AUGUSTINE

The acid test of our faith in the promises of God
is never found in the easy-going, comfortable
ways of life, but in the great emergencies,
the times of storm and of stress, the days of
adversity, when all human aid fails.

ETHEL BELL

Faith sees the invisible, believes the
unbelievable, and receives the impossible.

CORRIE TEN BOOM

*"For I the L*ORD *do not change; therefore you,
O children of Jacob, are not consumed."*

MALACHI 3:6 ESV

*And without faith it is impossible to please
Him, for he who comes to God must believe
that He is and that He is a rewarder
of those who seek Him.*

HEBREWS 11:6 NASB

*"The Rock! His work is perfect, for all His ways
are just; a God of faithfulness and without
injustice, righteous and upright is He."*

DEUTERONOMY 32:4 NASB

Unwavering Faithfulness

Father, Your faithfulness never wavers. When someone treats *me* unfairly, I feel my blood begin to boil. I give the cold shoulder. I am civil but not kind. I am not faithful even to You, my God. I question my faith when bad things happen. You are faithful even when I turn away. And when I am ready to return to Your arms, You never ask why it took me so long. You are just glad I have returned. Thank You for Your faithfulness. Make me faithful to You, I pray.

"Bring the full tithe into the storehouse, that there
may be food in my house. And thereby put me to
the test, says the Lord of hosts, if I will not open
the windows of heaven for you and pour down for
you a blessing until there is no more need."

MALACHI 3:10 ESV

O Lord, You are my God; I will exalt You,
I will give thanks to Your name; for You
have worked wonders, plans formed
long ago, with perfect faithfulness.

ISAIAH 25:1 NASB

Faith is not believing that God can,
it is knowing that he will.

UNKNOWN

Oftentimes God demonstrates His faithfulness
in adversity by providing for us what we need
to survive. He does not change our painful
circumstances. He sustains us through them.

CHARLES STANLEY

From the tiny birds of the air and from the
fragile lilies of the field, we learn the same
truth. . .God takes care of His own. . . . At just
the right moment, He steps in and proves
Himself as our faithful heavenly Father.

CHARLES SWINDOLL

Therefore, those also who suffer according to the will of God shall entrust their souls to a faithful Creator in doing what is right.

1 PETER 4:19 NASB

And we know that the Son of God has come, and has given us understanding so that we may know Him who is true; and we are in Him who is true, in His Son Jesus Christ. This is the true God and eternal life.

1 JOHN 5:20 NASB

O LORD God of Heaven's Armies! Where is there anyone as mighty as you, O LORD? You are entirely faithful.

PSALM 89:8 NLT

The Father's Touch

As I come before You, casting my disappointments
at Your feet, I feel the touch of Your hand upon
my weary brow. You embrace me in Your strong
arms and remind me that I am Yours. You take
the last worry from my tight grasp, wipe away
my tears. Like a parent returning his child to
the playground after tending to a scraped knee,
You return me to life with a kiss to make it better.

God is not an employer looking for employees.
He is an Eagle looking for people who will take
refuge under His wings. He is looking for people
who will leave father and mother and homeland
or anything else that may hold them back from
a life of love under the wings of Jesus.

JOHN PIPER

Remember: He wants your fellowship, and He
has done everything possible to make it a reality.
He has forgiven your sins, at the cost of His own
dear Son. He has given you His Word, and the
priceless privilege of prayer and worship.

BILLY GRAHAM

He Knows
Your Weaknesses

A final word: Be strong in the Lord and in his mighty power.

EPHESIANS 6:10 NLT

From prison, the apostle Paul wrote to the church at Ephesus instructing the people on how to live God-honoring lives. The letter is packed with insights including teaching on salvation by grace through faith in Christ alone. As Paul concluded this important letter, which some scholars believe was distributed to several early churches, he chose these words:

> *"Finally, be strong in the Lord and in his mighty power."* NIV

The famous reference to the "full armor of God" comes next. Paul warns that the believers' fight is not against this world but rather against evil spiritual forces of the heavenly realm.

Paul was aware that the early Christians were weak. He himself was weak. His only "super power" came directly from God. Paul knew from whom his strength came, and he carefully laid out the necessities for the Ephesians to tap into this same strength. The *belt of truth, breastplate of righteousness, feet fitted with the gospel of peace, shield of faith, helmet of salvation and sword of the Spirit* were—and are—essentials! Christians today should heed Paul's advice. God has provided us with His Word and with the privilege of prayer. We are weak, but in Jesus we are strong!

Next time you part ways with a fellow Christian, consider admonishing him or her in the way Paul did the Ephesians. Encourage your friend to *"Be strong in the Lord!"*

But he said to me, "My grace is sufficient for you, for my power is made perfect in weakness." Therefore I will boast all the more gladly of my weaknesses, so that the power of Christ may rest upon me.

2 CORINTHIANS 12:9 ESV

"Blessed are the poor in spirit, for theirs is the kingdom of heaven. Blessed are those who mourn, for they shall be comforted. Blessed are the gentle, for they shall inherit the earth."

MATTHEW 5:3–5 NASB

For all have sinned and fall short of the glory of God.

ROMANS 3:23 ESV

Savior Strength

Lord Jesus, I am weak but You are strong.
I sang the song as a little child, and how true
I have learned it is! I gain strength to persevere
through my relationship with You. How do
nonbelievers make it in this life? They must
be so depleted of energy and joy at all times.
I am blessed to be replenished daily with a
dose of my Savior's strength! Thank You,
Jesus, for strengthening me.

Many a humble soul will be amazed to find
that the seed that is sowed in weakness, in the
dust of daily life, has blossomed into immortal
flowers under the eye of the Lord.

HARRIET BEECHER STOWE

The child of God ought to confess his weakness
that he does not know how to pray, and petition
the Holy Spirit to teach him.

WATCHMAN NEE

Deny your weakness, and you will
never realize God's strength in you.

JONI EARECKSON TADA

Real true faith is man's weakness
leaning on God's strength.

D. L. MOODY

*O LORD, do not stay far away! You are
my strength; come quickly to my aid!*
PSALM 22:19 NLT

*But LORD, be merciful to us, for we have
waited for you. Be our strong arm each
day and our salvation in times of trouble.*
ISAIAH 33:2 NLT

*I pray that from his glorious, unlimited
resources he will empower you with
inner strength through his Spirit.*
EPHESIANS 3:16 NLT

In the same way, the Spirit helps us in our weakness. We do not know what we ought to pray for, but the Spirit himself intercedes for us through wordless groans.

ROMANS 8:26 NIV

And he told them a parable to the effect that they ought always to pray and not lose heart.

LUKE 18:1 ESV

"I the LORD search the heart and test the mind, to give every man according to his ways, according to the fruit of his deeds."

JEREMIAH 17:10 ESV

You Are My Strength

Father, I am drowning. You are my life
preserver. I am sinking. You lift me up. I
stumble. You make my path straight. I slip.
You steady me. In all my weakness, You are
strong. I don't have to be strong enough or good
enough or brave enough. I just have to pray.
When I call out to You, You come running.
Thank You for being my strength. Amen.

"Give justice to the weak and the fatherless;
maintain the right of the afflicted and the
destitute. Rescue the weak and the needy;
deliver them from the hand of the wicked."

PSALM 82:3–4 ESV

"Watch and pray that you may not enter
into temptation. The spirit indeed is
willing, but the flesh is weak."

MATTHEW 26:41 ESV

Life is war. That's not all it is. But it is always
that. Our weakness in prayer is owing largely
to our neglect of this truth. Prayer is primarily
a wartime walkie-talkie for the mission of the
church as it advances against the powers
of darkness and unbelief.

JOHN PIPER

When we pray for the Spirit's help. . .we
will simply fall down at the Lord's feet in
our weakness. There we will find the victory
and power that comes from His love.

ANDREW MURRAY

*For we do not have a high priest who is
unable to empathize with our weaknesses,
but we have one who has been tempted in
every way, just as we are—yet he did not sin.*

HEBREWS 4:15 NIV

*That is why, for Christ's sake, I delight
in weaknesses, in insults, in hardships,
in persecutions, in difficulties. For when
I am weak, then I am strong.*

2 CORINTHIANS 12:10 NIV

*For God has not given us a spirit of fear,
but of power and of love and of a sound mind.*

2 TIMOTHY 1:7 NKJV

Refuge in Christ

So God has given both his promise and his oath. These two things are unchangeable because it is impossible for God to lie. Therefore, we who have fled to him for refuge can have great confidence as we hold to the hope that lies before us. This hope is a strong and trustworthy anchor for our souls. It leads us through the curtain into God's inner sanctuary.

HEBREWS 6:18–19 NLT

A curtain separated man from the holiest part of the temple. When Jesus took His last breath on the cross and submitted His spirit to the Father, the curtain was torn. It was torn from top to bottom. Everything changed in that instant.

Sinners may enter into the presence of Almighty God through the blood of Jesus, the perfect sacrifice. He gives us access to our holy God. Without Him, we would be separated from God.

Stand firm in this life. Cling to God through your faith in Christ. Recognize your salvation as a wonderful refuge from this dark and dangerous world. Like a boat at sea held steady by an anchor, you are anchored in Christ. He is a strong anchor. Otherwise, certainly the strong winds would carry you away. The prince of this world is a dark being. Satan would love nothing more than to see you tossing and turning upon the waves of life, adrift from the shore with no port, no home, no haven in which to rest. But you do not belong to this world. Nor do you belong to the evil one. Your hope is found in nothing less than the blood of the Son of the Most High. Make Jesus your refuge. Ask Him to protect you and to hold you close. He is the only true security.

Trust in him at all times, O people;
pour out your heart before him;
God is a refuge for us. Selah.

PSALM 62:8 ESV

God is our refuge and strength,
an ever-present help in trouble.

PSALM 46:1 NIV

"The LORD repay your work, and a full reward
be given you by the LORD God of Israel, under
whose wings you have come for refuge."

RUTH 2:12 NKJV

The LORD also will be a refuge for the
oppressed, a refuge in times of trouble.

PSALM 9:9 NKJV

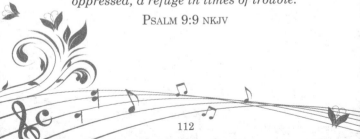

Because God has made us for Himself, our
hearts are restless until they rest in Him.

AUGUSTINE OF HIPPO

Where does your security lie? Is God your
refuge, your hiding place, your stronghold, your
shepherd, your counselor, your friend, your
redeemer, your savior, your guide? If He is, you
don't need to search any further for security.

ELISABETH ELLIOT

Our "safe place" is not where
we live, it is in whom we live.

TOM WHITE

I am going out on Thy path. God be behind me,
God be before, God be in my footsteps.

GAELIC PRAYER

The LORD is their strength, and He
is the saving refuge of His anointed.

PSALM 28:8 NKJV

"The God of my strength, in whom I will trust;
my shield and the horn of my salvation, my
stronghold and my refuge; my Savior,
You save me from violence."

2 SAMUEL 22:3 NKJV

But I will sing of Your power; yes, I will
sing aloud of Your mercy in the morning;
for You have been my defense and
refuge in the day of my trouble.

PSALM 59:16 NKJV

A Mighty Fortress

Lord Jesus, hold me close. There is nowhere on earth I feel safer than in Your arms. I don't want to be independent. I want to learn to live life completely dependent on You, my Savior. You are my refuge. You provide the security that I need in order to walk in this world. There are evil spiritual forces at work, but with the Son of God as my fortress, I have nothing to fear. Amen.

I have become as a wonder to many,
but You are my strong refuge.
PSALM 71:7 NKJV

But my eyes are upon You, O GOD the Lord; in
You I take refuge; do not leave my soul destitute.
PSALM 141:8 NKJV

Those who fear the LORD are secure;
he will be a refuge for their children.
PROVERBS 14:26 NLT

"It is God who arms me with
strength and keeps my way secure."
2 SAMUEL 22:33 NIV

When the devil knocks at the door of my heart, I take Jesus by the hand. I ask Him to go with me to answer the door. When I open the door, the devil sees me and Jesus standing hand in hand and he says, "Excuse me, I must be at the wrong place."

HERBERT C. GABHART

I cannot make myself a refuge, but Jesus has provided it, His Father has given it, His Spirit has revealed it, and lo, again tonight I enter it, and am safe from every foe.

CHARLES SPURGEON

*He is my loving ally and my fortress, my tower
of safety, my rescuer. He is my shield, and I take
refuge in him. He makes the nations submit to me.*

PSALM 144:2 NLT

*For You have been a strength to the poor, a
strength to the needy in his distress, a refuge from
the storm, a shade from the heat; for the blast of
the terrible ones is as a storm against the wall.*

ISAIAH 25:4 NKJV

*The LORD is their strength, and He
is the saving refuge of His anointed.*

PSALM 28:8 NKJV

Security in Jesus

During your ministry on earth, Lord, You
sought out the underdog. The tax collector.
The prostitute. The leper. You formed
relationships with those who needed a safety
net, a place to fall, a refuge. Be my refuge,
Lord Jesus. I need a haven, a sense of security.
Thank You for promising that You will never
leave or forsake me, Jesus.

"But whoever listens to me will dwell safely, and will be secure, without fear of evil."

PROVERBS 1:33 NKJV

In God is my salvation and my glory; the rock of my strength, and my refuge, is in God.

PSALM 62:7 NKJV

Our soul waits for the LORD;
He is our help and our shield.

PSALM 33:20 NKJV

Some trust in chariots, and some in horses; but we will remember the name of the LORD our God.

PSALM 20:7 NKJV

In Jesus the weak are strong, and the defenseless safe; they could not be more strong if they were giants, or more safe if they were in heaven.

CHARLES SPURGEON

How happy would you be if your hearts were but persuaded to close with Jesus Christ! Then you would be out of all danger: whatever storms and tempests were without, you might rest securely within; you might hear the rushing of the wind, and the thunder roar abroad, while you are safe in this hiding-place. O be persuaded to hide yourself in Christ Jesus!

JONATHAN EDWARDS

*Bring to an end the violence of the wicked and
make the righteous secure—you, the righteous
God who probes minds and hearts.*

PSALM 7:9 NIV

*I keep my eyes always on the LORD. With him
at my right hand, I will not be shaken. Therefore
my heart is glad and my tongue rejoices; my
body also will rest secure, because you will not
abandon me to the realm of the dead, nor will
you let your faithful one see decay.*

PSALM 16:8–10 NIV

Forsaken by Others

"As for you, you meant evil against me, but God meant it for good in order to bring about this present result, to preserve many people alive."

GENESIS 50:20 NASB

Joseph understood being forsaken by others. His own brothers sold him into slavery. They were jealous and wanted him out of their lives. But that is not how the story ends. . . .

Joseph wound up in Egypt and thus, a fascinating turn of events crafted by the providential hand of God began. Joseph became the personal attendant of Potiphar, a very important official of Pharoah, the ruler of Egypt. He then spent years in prison for a crime he did not commit when Potiphar's wife told awful lies about him. But eventually Joseph was released, finding favor with Pharoah by interpreting his dreams.

Joseph, who was once sold into slavery on the side of the road, landed the position of prime minister of Egypt!

When Joseph's brothers appeared before him again years later, they didn't recognize him. There was a great famine in Israel. Their father, Jacob, sent them to buy grain in Egypt. After a test, Joseph determined that his brothers' cold hearts had changed. They feared him when he said, "I am Joseph." But they had nothing to fear. Joseph forgave them. He told them to gather all their relatives and come to Egypt where he provided land. God used Joseph to save the nation of Israel from which the Messiah would come. What others meant for evil, God used for good.

When others forsake you, look to God. He will always be with you, and He will use even the deepest hurts in your life for good.

*Those who hate me without cause outnumber
the hairs on my head. Many enemies try to
destroy me with lies, demanding that
I give back what I didn't steal.*

PSALM 69:4 NLT

*Rescue me from the mud; don't let me sink any
deeper! Save me from those who hate me, and
pull me from these deep waters. Don't let the
floods overwhelm me, or the deep waters swallow
me, or the pit of death devour me.*

PSALM 69:14–15 NLT

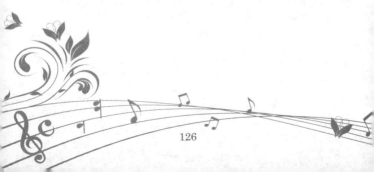

Friendship is like a glass ornament,
once it is broken it can rarely be put
back together exactly the same way.

CHARLES KINGSLEY

I went out to find a friend,
But could not find one there.
I went out to be a friend,
And friends were everywhere!

UNKNOWN

If you live for any joy on earth,
you may be forsaken; but, oh, live for Jesus,
and he will never forsake you!

MATTHEW SIMPSON

*But as for me, I will look to the L*ORD*;*
I will wait for the God of my salvation;
my God will hear me.

MICAH 7:7 ESV

The poor are shunned by all their relatives—
how much more do their friends avoid them!
Though the poor pursue them with pleading,
they are nowhere to be found.

PROVERBS 19:7 NIV

"No one will be able to stand against you all the
days of your life. As I was with Moses, so I will be
with you; I will never leave you nor forsake you."

JOSHUA 1:5 NIV

Others Let Me Down

Other people let me down, Father. I know that I
let them down as well. It is part of being human!
But You are faithful even when my friends turn
away. Sometimes I go through my list of friends
and it seems no one wants to spend time with
me. I become discouraged. But then I remember
that You are always there. You are my most
faithful friend. I love You, Lord.

*"May the Lord our God be with us as
he was with our ancestors; may he
never leave us nor forsake us."*

1 Kings 8:57 niv

*Do not hide your face from me, do not turn your
servant away in anger; you have been my helper.
Do not reject me or forsake me, God my Savior.*

Psalm 27:9 niv

*Once I was young, and now I am old.
Yet I have never seen the godly abandoned
or their children begging for bread.*

Psalm 37:25 nlt

Truly great friends are hard to find,
difficult to leave, and impossible to forget.

G. RANDOLF

Your greatest ministry will most likely
come out of your greatest hurt.

RICK WARREN

I destroy my enemies when
I make them my friends.

ABRAHAM LINCOLN

"For Israel and Judah have not been forsaken by
their God, the LORD Almighty, though their land
is full of guilt before the Holy One of Israel."

JEREMIAH 51:5 NIV

"As for me, I know that my Redeemer lives, and
at the last He will take His stand on the earth."

JOB 19:25 NASB

Our ancestors trusted in you, and you rescued
them. They cried out to you and were saved.
They trusted in you and were never disgraced.

PSALM 22:4–5 NLT

God Is Faithful

God, I read in the Bible about men and
women to whom You were faithful. You told
Noah to build an ark before the flood. You
led the Israelites out of bondage. You gave
Abraham a son in old age. I know that You are
the Great I Am, the same yesterday, today,
and forever. Help me to trust in Your great
faithfulness to Your children. Remind me of
Your deep love for me, I pray. Amen.

"Behold, God is mighty but does not despise any;
He is mighty in strength of understanding."
JOB 36:5 NASB

"Do not forsake wisdom, and she will protect
you; love her, and she will watch over you."
PROVERBS 4:6 NIV

If an enemy were insulting me, I could endure
it; if a foe were rising against me, I could hide.
But it is you, a man like myself, my companion,
my close friend, with whom I once enjoyed sweet
fellowship at the house of God, as we walked
about among the worshipers.
PSALM 55:12–14 NIV

Shield and Solace

Blessed be the God and Father of our Lord Jesus Christ, the Father of mercies and God of all comfort, who comforts us in all our tribulation, that we may be able to comfort those who are in any trouble, with the comfort with which we ourselves are comforted by God.

2 CORINTHIANS 1:3–4 NKJV

"God does not comfort us to make us comfortable only, but to make us comforters," Dr. John Henry J. H. Jowett once said. He was an English pastor who served also as pastor of a New York church. People lined up to hear his sermons regardless of the fact that he read aloud as he preached. Why? It was because the truths were biblical and right on target.

This is one of those truths: God comforts us so that we might comfort others. Dr. Jowett did not create it. He taught it directly from the Bible.

Once you have known the comfort of God, you will want to pass it on. When the Lord Himself has carried you through a dark and frightening trial and you reach the other side, you will never miss an opportunity to comfort someone facing a similar struggle. If you have experienced the loss of a parent, a child, or a marriage, look around for those who are in the same boat. If you have been comforted when you lost your way and had to make your way back to God, it won't be hard to find another soul battling the same sin or addiction. God comforts that we might comfort others. If you have found solace in the loving arms of the Lord, lead another to those same safe arms. Go therefore into your hurting world and. . .pass it on.

"God's way is perfect. All the LORD's promises prove true. He is a shield for all who look to him for protection."

2 SAMUEL 22:31 NLT

But you, O LORD, are a shield around me; you are my glory, the one who holds my head high.

PSALM 3:3 NLT

For you bless the godly, O LORD; you surround them with your shield of love.

PSALM 5:12 NLT

My shield is God Most High, who saves the upright in heart.

PSALM 7:10 NIV

Jesus feels for thee; Jesus consoles thee;
Jesus will help thee.

CHARLES SPURGEON

If a child is in its father's arms, nothing
can touch it without that father's consent,
unless he is too weak to prevent it. And even
if this should be the case, he suffers the harm
first in his own person before he allows it to
reach his child. If an earthly parent would thus
care for his little helpless one, how much more
will our heavenly Father, whose love is infinitely
greater and whose strength and wisdom
can never be baffled, care for us!

HANNAH WHITALL SMITH

"You have given me your shield of victory;
your help has made me great."

2 SAMUEL 22:36 NLT

*Therefore if there is any encouragement in
Christ, if there is any consolation of love, if there
is any fellowship of the Spirit, if any affection
and compassion, make my joy complete by being
of the same mind, maintaining the same love,
united in spirit, intent on one purpose.*

PHILIPPIANS 2:1–2 NASB

I Run to You

When it seems that no one understands me
or when my world is turned upside down,
I run to You. I find solace and comfort in
Your arms, heavenly Father. You shield me
from the pressures of the world and set me
straight upon the path again. You point me in
the right direction. You remind me that You
are always just a prayer away. Amen.

The Lord is my rock, my fortress, and my savior;
my God is my rock, in whom I find protection.
He is my shield, the power that saves me,
and my place of safety.

Psalm 18:2 NLT

God's way is perfect. All the Lord's promises
prove true. He is a shield for all who
look to him for protection.

Psalm 18:30 NLT

The Lord is my strength and my shield;
my heart trusted in Him, and I am helped;
therefore my heart greatly rejoices,
and with my song I will praise Him.

Psalm 28:7 NKJV

You don't have to be alone in your hurt!
Comfort is yours. Joy is an option. And it's
all been made possible by Your Savior. He
went without comfort so you might have it.
He postponed joy so you might share in it. He
willingly chose isolation so you might never be
alone in your hurt and sorrow.

JONI EARECKSON TADA

Pray often; for prayer is a shield to the soul,
a sacrifice to God, and a scourge for Satan.

JOHN BUNYAN

God never gives strength for tomorrow,
or for the next hour, but only for
the strain of the minute.

OSWALD CHAMBERS

*Put on your armor, and take up your shield.
Prepare for battle, and come to my aid.*

PSALM 35:2 NLT

*For the LORD God is our sun and our shield. He
gives us grace and glory. The LORD will withhold
no good thing from those who do what is right.*

PSALM 84:11 NLT

*When my anxious thoughts multiply within me,
Your consolations delight my soul.*

PSALM 94:19 NASB

The Great I Am

Lord, You are my shield. You defend me. You are
my solace. You give me rest. You are the Great
I Am. You stand ready to help in any situation.
Like a parent who knows each type of cry his
child makes, You know me. You are at times my
Prince of Peace and at other times, my Jehovah-
Jireh, "the Lord my Protector." Thank You, Lord,
for being my shield and my solace. Amen.

*Now may the God of patience and comfort
grant you to be like-minded toward one another,
according to Christ Jesus, that you may with
one mind and one mouth glorify the God and
Father of our Lord Jesus Christ.*
ROMANS 15:5–6 NKJV

*When anxiety was great within me,
your consolation brought me joy.*
PSALM 94:19 NIV

*You who are my Comforter in sorrow,
my heart is faint within me.*
JEREMIAH 8:18 NIV

The Savior's Promise

Praise be to the LORD, to God our Savior,
who daily bears our burdens.

PSALM 68:19 NIV

Jesus promises to bear our burdens. What kind
of friend does that? Certainly some friends will
walk alongside us, but none except Jesus is
able to take our burden from us. He calls to you
and asks you to lay down your heavy load. He
says to cast your cares upon Him because He
is strong and He can handle all your worries.
He cares for you. He declares that nothing will
be able to snatch you out of the Father's hand.
Nothing. Not angels or demons. Not anything
past, present, or future. Once you are saved
by the blood of Jesus, it covers you, gives you
a new name, and secures your position before
Almighty God. You are righteous through that
blood. You are God's beloved child, adopted
through grace and unconditionally loved.

So why worry and fret? Why grow anxious about your current situation or needlessly stay up at night contemplating an unknown future? Run to Christ. He is ready and willing to take all your burdens upon Himself. He is not just the classmate who offers to carry your books or backpack for a while. Eventually, the classmate returns the load. Not so with Jesus! He is the Son of the Living God. He wants to cast those burdens as far as the east is from the west and replace them with peace and joy and contentment. He is your blessed Messiah. He wants to see you laugh and rejoice again. Give it all to Jesus. And don't look back.

Stand fast therefore in the liberty by which
Christ has made us free, and do not be
entangled again with a yoke of bondage.

GALATIANS 5:1 NKJV

We are hard-pressed on every side,
yet not crushed; we are perplexed,
but not in despair; persecuted, but not
forsaken; struck down, but not destroyed.

2 CORINTHIANS 4:8–9 NKJV

I will lift up my eyes to the hills—
from whence comes my help? My help comes
from the LORD, who made heaven and earth.

PSALM 121:1–2 NKJV

When an answer I did not expect comes to a prayer which I believed I truly meant, I shrink back from it; if the burden my Lord asks me to bear be not the burden of my heart's choice, and I fret inwardly and do not welcome His will, then I know nothing of Calvary love.

AMY CARMICHAEL

Only good things come from God's hands. He never gives you more than you can bear. Every burden prepares you for eternity.

BASILEA SCHLINK

Any concern too small to be turned into a prayer is too small to be made into a burden.

CORRIE TEN BOOM

Bear one another's burdens,
and thereby fulfill the law of Christ.

GALATIANS 6:2 NASB

"I will take you to be my people, and I will be
your God, and you shall know that I am the
LORD your God, who has brought you out from
under the burdens of the Egyptians."

EXODUS 6:7 ESV

"Take My yoke upon you and learn from Me,
for I am gentle and lowly in heart, and you
will find rest for your souls. For My yoke
is easy and My burden is light."

MATTHEW 11:29–30 NKJV

Surrendering Burdens to Christ

Oh Jesus, You say that You will gladly bear my
burdens for me. But so often I resist Your offer.
I stay up all night worrying about the future
when my future is secure in You. I worry about
tomorrow when, as the Bible says, it has enough
trouble of its own. I want to surrender my cares
to You. Take them, Jesus. Help me to surrender,
I ask. Help me to trust You. Amen.

For this is the love of God, that we keep His commandments; and His commandments are not burdensome.

1 JOHN 5:3 NASB

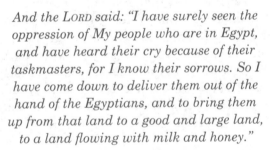

And the LORD said: "I have surely seen the oppression of My people who are in Egypt, and have heard their cry because of their taskmasters, for I know their sorrows. So I have come down to deliver them out of the hand of the Egyptians, and to bring them up from that land to a good and large land, to a land flowing with milk and honey."

EXODUS 3:7–8 NKJV

None knows the weight of another's burden.
GEORGE HERBERT

Abide in Me, says Jesus. Cling to Me. Stick fast to Me. Live the life of close and intimate communion with Me. Get nearer to Me. Roll every burden on Me. Cast your whole weight on Me. Never let go your hold on Me for a moment. Be, as it were, rooted and planted in Me. Do this and I will never fail you. I will ever abide in you.

J. C. RYLE

He is despised and rejected by men, a Man of
sorrows and acquainted with grief. And we
hid, as it were, our faces from Him; He was
despised, and we did not esteem Him. Surely He
has borne our griefs and carried our sorrows;
yet we esteemed Him stricken, smitten by God,
and afflicted. But He was wounded for our
transgressions, He was bruised for our iniquities;
the chastisement for our peace was upon Him,
and by His stripes we are healed.

Isaiah 53:3–5 NKJV

Releasing My Worries

When I release my worries, You replace them
with laughter. I love to laugh, Lord. I catch a
glimpse of my face in the mirror and I see a
lighter me. Thank You for carrying my burdens.
Thank You for relieving me of the great
pressure that I was not meant to bear—the
pressure of figuring it all out, the stress
of plotting and planning. You are in control.
I like it that way!

As for the saints who are on the earth, "They are the excellent ones, in whom is all my delight." Their sorrows shall be multiplied who hasten after another god; their drink offerings of blood I will not offer, nor take up their names on my lips.

PSALM 16:3–4 NKJV

Many sorrows shall be to the wicked; but he who trusts in the LORD, mercy shall surround him.

PSALM 32:10 NKJV

Earnest Prayer

You, God, are my God, earnestly I seek you;
I thirst for you, my whole being longs for you,
in a dry and parched land where there is no water.

PSALM 63:1 NIV

Earnest prayers. They fill the pages of the
Bible. Jonah prayed from the belly of the great
fish. Hannah cried out in anguish for a child.
Elijah, wanting to prove the strength of the
one true God, prayed for fire. David prayed for
forgiveness when he had committed adultery.
Jesus, the very Son of God, prayed so furiously
in the Garden of Gethsemane that His sweat
turned to blood. Have you prayed earnestly to
the Lord for a need in your life? Prayer is the
way that you make known to God what you need
and desire.

God does not always answer prayers the way we think He should. But He is faithful to answer the prayers of His children. Sometimes the answer is yes. Other times it is no. The Father may answer your prayer now. He may require you to wait for some of your prayers to be answered.

Imagine walking through a desert. You have no water and the sun beats down on you, draining you of all strength. Suddenly you see a lush waterfall pouring into a glistening lake. Wouldn't you run to it and quench your thirst? Certainly you would not only drink from it but plunge into the water, refreshing your weary body. Seek your heavenly Father in prayer in this same manner. Seek Him earnestly. He will refresh your spirit.

*Hear my prayer, O Lord, give ear to
my supplications! In Your faithfulness
answer me, and in Your righteousness.*

Psalm 143:1 nkjv

*Continue earnestly in prayer,
being vigilant in it with thanksgiving.*

Colossians 4:2 nkjv

*What other nation is so great as to have their
gods near them the way the Lord our God
is near us whenever we pray to him?*

Deuteronomy 4:7 niv

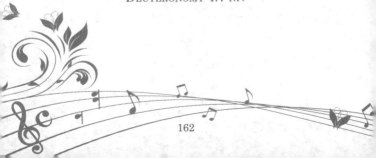

Our prayers may be awkward. Our attempts may be feeble. But since the power of prayer is in the one who hears it and not in the one who says it, our prayers do make a difference.

Max Lucado

Can Jesus Christ see the agony of His soul in us? He can't unless we are so closely identified with Him that we have His view concerning the people for whom we pray. May we learn to intercede so wholeheartedly that Jesus Christ will be completely and overwhelmingly satisfied with us as intercessors.

Oswald Chambers

*Therefore confess your sins to each other
and pray for each other so that you may
be healed. The prayer of a righteous
person is powerful and effective.*

JAMES 5:16 NIV

*"But if you will seek God earnestly and plead
with the Almighty, if you are pure and upright,
even now he will rouse himself on your behalf
and restore you to your prosperous state."*

JOB 8:5–6 NIV

*Isaac prayed to the LORD on behalf of his
wife, because she was childless. The LORD
answered his prayer, and his wife
Rebekah became pregnant.*

GENESIS 25:21 NIV

Drive-By Prayer

Lord, sometimes I attempt the drive-by prayer.
It is something like cruising through a fast-
food restaurant for a burger. I hardly stop. I
whisper a prayer and then am easily distracted
by technology or a friend. Surely You hear my
prayers as I drive down the road or go about my
day. But help me to set aside time for earnest
prayer. I know that You want all of me. Amen.

And without faith it is impossible to please God, because anyone who comes to him must believe that he exists and that he rewards those who earnestly seek him.

HEBREWS 11:6 NIV

Elijah was a human being, even as we are. He prayed earnestly that it would not rain, and it did not rain on the land for three and a half years. Again he prayed, and the heavens gave rain, and the earth produced its crops.

JAMES 5:17–18 NIV

So we fasted and earnestly prayed that our God would take care of us, and he heard our prayer.

EZRA 8:23 NLT

Those who know God the best are the richest
and most powerful in prayer. Little acquaintance
with God, and strangeness and coldness to Him,
make prayer a rare and feeble thing.

EDWARD MCKENDREE BOUNDS

Heaven is full of answers to prayer
for which no one ever bothered to ask.

BILLY GRAHAM

Prayer is exhaling the spirit of man
and inhaling the spirit of God.

EDWIN KEITH

Our prayers lay the track down on which
God's power can come. Like a mighty
locomotive, his power is irresistible,
but it cannot reach us without rails.

WATCHMAN NEE

And He was withdrawn from them about a stone's throw, and He knelt down and prayed, saying, "Father, if it is Your will, take this cup away from Me; nevertheless not My will, but Yours, be done." Then an angel appeared to Him from heaven, strengthening Him. And being in agony, He prayed more earnestly. Then His sweat became like great drops of blood falling down to the ground.

LUKE 22:41–44 NKJV

So in the course of time Hannah became pregnant and gave birth to a son. She named him Samuel, saying, "Because I asked the LORD for him."

1 SAMUEL 1:20 NIV

With My Whole Heart

Lord, You tell me in Your Word that the earnest
prayer of a righteous man is effective. I know
that I have been made righteous through the
blood of Christ. I can come before You even
though You are a holy God. I can enter into Your
presence through Jesus. What grace You have
poured out on me! What a privilege is prayer!
I seek You now with my whole heart. Amen.

*"Yet give attention to your servant's prayer
and his plea for mercy, Lord my God.
Hear the cry and the prayer that your
servant is praying in your presence this day."*
1 Kings 8:28 NIV

*When Elisha reached the house, there was
the boy lying dead on his couch. He went in,
shut the door on the two of them and prayed
to the Lord. Then he got on the bed and lay
on the boy, mouth to mouth, eyes to eyes,
hands to hands. As he stretched himself out
on him, the boy's body grew warm.*
2 Kings 4:32–34 NIV

No Need for Prayer in Glory

"He will wipe every tear from their eyes. There will be no more death or mourning or crying or pain, for the old order of things has passed away."

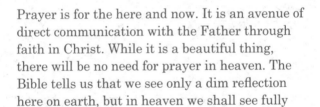

Prayer is for the here and now. It is an avenue of direct communication with the Father through faith in Christ. While it is a beautiful thing, there will be no need for prayer in heaven. The Bible tells us that we see only a dim reflection here on earth, but in heaven we shall see fully even as we are fully known by God.

On this earth, we have longings. We have unmet desires. We think we need a lot of things. Really, we only need God. One day, when we are in His glorious kingdom, we will understand. We won't need to carry our burdens to Jesus any longer. There will be no more burdens. We won't cry any more tears. The Word of God declares that there will be no tears in heaven. How can it be that there will be no more grief? There will be no more grief because there will be no more death. Pain will not exist. You will have a new body. Imagine it! You know those little aches? You know those parts of your earthly body that don't work quite right? They will trouble you no longer. You will have a spiritual body. While heaven remains a mystery, we know that Jesus says it will be joyous there. Eternal happiness. So pray while you are here on this earth. Walk with God through prayer. One day you will see your Father face-to-face!

But our citizenship is in heaven. And we eagerly await a Savior from there, the Lord Jesus Christ, who, by the power that enables him to bring everything under his control, will transform our lowly bodies so that they will be like his glorious body.

PHILIPPIANS 3:20–21 NIV

For the Lord himself will come down from heaven, with a loud command, with the voice of the archangel and with the trumpet call of God, and the dead in Christ will rise first.

1 THESSALONIANS 4:16 NIV

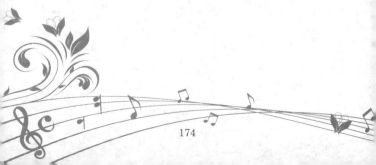

We talk about heaven being so far away.
It is within speaking distance to those
who belong there. Heaven is a prepared
place for a prepared people.

D. L. Moody

Joy is the serious business of heaven.

C. S. Lewis

To go to heaven, fully to enjoy God,
is infinitely better than the most
pleasant accommodations here.

Jonathan Edwards

I would not give one moment of heaven for all
the joy and riches of the world, even if it lasted
for thousands and thousands of years.

Martin Luther

But in keeping with his promise we are looking
forward to a new heaven and a new earth,
where righteousness dwells.

2 PETER 3:13 NIV

The heavens declare the glory of God;
and the firmament shows His handiwork.

PSALM 19:1 NKJV

"Therefore rejoice, you heavens and you who
dwell in them! But woe to the earth and the
sea, because the devil has gone down to you!
He is filled with fury, because he knows
that his time is short."

REVELATION 12:12 NIV

Looking Forward to Heaven

Lord Jesus, You are preparing a place for me
in heaven. You know the day and the time that
I will enter that glorious kingdom. It is not for
me to know. Heaven is mysterious. There are so
many things I don't know or understand about
it. But I understand that it will be beautiful.
I look forward to heaven!

Then I heard a voice from heaven say, "Write this:
Blessed are the dead who die in the Lord from
now on." "Yes," says the Spirit, "they will rest
from their labor, for their deeds will follow them."
REVELATION 14:13 NIV

"In My Father's house are many mansions; if it
were not so, I would have told you. I go to prepare
a place for you. And if I go and prepare a place
for you, I will come again and receive you to
Myself; that where I am, there you may be also."
JOHN 14:2–3 NKJV

God destines us for an end
beyond the grasp of reason.

THOMAS AQUINAS

The best we can hope for in this life is a
knothole peek at the shining realities ahead.
Yet a glimpse is enough. It's enough to convince
our hearts that whatever sufferings and sorrows
currently assail us aren't worthy of comparison
to that which waits over the horizon.

JONI EARECKSON TADA

I can safely say, on the authority of all that is
revealed in the Word of God, that any man or
woman on this earth who is bored and turned
off by worship is not ready for heaven.

A. W. TOZER

*The heavens are Yours, the earth also
is Yours; the world and all its fullness,
You have founded them.*

PSALM 89:11 NKJV

*Unto You I lift up my eyes,
O You who dwell in the heavens.*

PSALM 123:1 NKJV

*Oh, give thanks to the God of heaven!
For His mercy endures forever.*

PSALM 136:26 NKJV

*O LORD, our Lord, how excellent is
Your name in all the earth, who have
set Your glory above the heavens!*

PSALM 8:1 NKJV

Only Light

The longer that I live on this earth, the more
I long for heaven. There is so much evil here
where Satan is allowed to roam. There is no
place for Satan in heaven. He gave that position
up long ago when he turned away from You,
God. I cannot imagine a place where there is not
even a hint of darkness but only light, light, and
more light. Come quickly, Lord Jesus! Amen.

"And I will give you the keys of the kingdom of heaven, and whatever you bind on earth will be bound in heaven, and whatever you loose on earth will be loosed in heaven."

MATTHEW 16:19 NKJV

But the other criminal protested, "Don't you fear God even when you have been sentenced to die? We deserve to die for our crimes, but this man hasn't done anything wrong." Then he said, "Jesus, remember me when you come into your Kingdom." And Jesus replied, "I assure you, today you will be with me in paradise."

LUKE 23:40–43 NLT

Jesus, Your Forever Friend

But in him it is always Yes. For all the promises of God find their Yes in him. That is why it is through him that we utter our Amen to God for his glory.

2 CORINTHIANS 1:19–20 ESV

When a southerner visits New York City, she often hears the phrase, "You're not from here, are you?" The slowness of a southern drawl is evidence that the Big Apple is not her home! Similarly, Earth is not our home. We are just passing through. Heaven is our home and we are heaven-bound.

The important things will last. The rest will not. Most of the things of earth are not lasting. Just the relationships. Just your walk with Jesus. He is eternal. Jesus of Nazareth is the same Jesus we find praying earnestly in the Garden of Gethsemane. He is the same Jesus who healed the sick and raised the dead to life in the years in between. And when the Father did not remove the cup, Jesus grasped it with all His might and drank deep of it. . .for all mankind. And as the rich, red blood of perfect sacrifice ran down His face, it saved us.

So what will you do with Jesus? Your answer is crucial. Choose to follow Christ. Let Him lead you down every path. Ask Him which way to turn at each crossroad. When He says to stop, stop. When He blesses the journey, run freely into it. Jesus never falters. He will never come up short or leave you stranded. He knows the way because He *is* the Way. He is a truer friend than any you will ever know on earth. As you wait for His sure return, keep singing: *"What a friend we have in Jesus. . . ."*

To God, alone wise, be glory through
Jesus Christ forever. Amen.

ROMANS 16:27 NKJV

Jesus Christ is the same
yesterday, today, and forever.

HEBREWS 13:8 NKJV

Now may the God of peace who brought up our
Lord Jesus from the dead, that great Shepherd
of the sheep, through the blood of the everlasting
covenant, make you complete in every good
work to do His will, working in you what is well
pleasing in His sight, through Jesus Christ,
to whom be glory forever and ever. Amen.

HEBREWS 13:20–21 NKJV

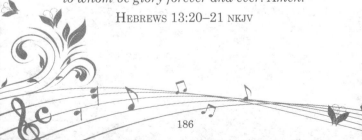

Endless Worship

Lord, one day I will praise You day and
night. For eternity I will worship You with
the angels and all the saints who have gone
before me. My portion will be sweet. On my
lips there will always be a song declaring
Your greatness. Let me taste of heaven on
this earth. Find me utterly surrendered to
You when I sing. Remove the distractions of
this world. May my focus be on You, Jesus.

*But grow in the grace and knowledge of
our Lord and Savior Jesus Christ. To Him
be the glory both now and forever. Amen.*

2 Peter 3:18 NKJV

*"And this is the way to have eternal life—
to know you, the only true God, and
Jesus Christ, the one you sent to earth."*

John 17:3 NLT

*For the wages of sin is death, but the
free gift of God is eternal life through
Christ Jesus our Lord.*

Romans 6:23 NLT

*This was his eternal plan, which he
carried out through Christ Jesus our Lord.*

Ephesians 3:11 NLT

Radical obedience to Christ is not easy. . . .
It's not comfort, not health, not wealth, and
not prosperity in this world. Radical obedience
to Christ risks losing all these things. But in
the end, such risk finds its reward in Christ.
And he is more than enough for us.

DAVID PLATT

We might be wise to follow the insight of the
enraptured heart rather than the more cautious
reasoning of the theological mind.

A. W. TOZER

In his kindness God called you to share in his eternal glory by means of Christ Jesus. So after you have suffered a little while, he will restore, support, and strengthen you, and he will place you on a firm foundation.

1 PETER 5:10 NLT

And whenever those possessed by evil spirits caught sight of him, the spirits would throw them to the ground in front of him shrieking, "You are the Son of God!"

MARK 3:11 NLT

Jesus Is Constant

Jesus, You are the constant in my changing life. You are always the same, always present, always loving. You left heaven for me and walked this earth long before I was born. You became fully man, even as You were still fully God. You are the way, the truth, and the life. No one comes to God except through You. I am so thankful that I know You. I love You, Jesus.

But you, dear friends, by building yourselves
up in your most holy faith and praying in the
Holy Spirit, keep yourselves in God's love as
you wait for the mercy of our Lord Jesus
Christ to bring you to eternal life.

JUDE 1:20–21 NIV

The disciples saw Jesus do many other
miraculous signs in addition to the ones recorded
in this book. But these are written so that you
may continue to believe that Jesus is the Messiah,
the Son of God, and that by believing in him
you will have life by the power of his name.

JOHN 20:30–31 NLT